BE A SCIENTIST!

Be a

PALEONTOLOGIST

BY LORI DOWELL

Gareth Stevens
PUBLISHING

Please visit our website, www.garethstevens.com. For a free color catalog of all our high-quality books, call toll free 1-800-542-2595 or fax 1-877-542-2596.

Library of Congress Cataloging-in-Publication Data

Dowell, Lori.
Be a paleontologist / by Lori Dowell.
p. cm. — (Be a scientist!)
Includes index.
ISBN 978-1-4824-1209-3 (pbk.)
ISBN 978-1-4824-1200-0 (6-pack)
ISBN 978-1-4824-1443-1 (library binding)
1. Paleontologists — Juvenile literature. 2. Paleontology — Vocational guidance — Juvenile literature. I. Title.
QE714.7 D69 2015
560—d23

First Edition

Published in 2015 by
Gareth Stevens Publishing
111 East 14th Street, Suite 349
New York, NY 10003

Designer: Katelyn E. Reynolds
Editor: Therese Shea

Photo credits: Cover, p. 1 Lowell Georgia/National Geographic/Getty Images; cover, pp. 1–32 (background texture) Kues/Shutterstock.com; p. 5 Marcio Silva/iStock/Thinkstock.com; pp. 7, 16 Natursports/Shutterstock.com; p. 8 Pasicles/Wikipedia.com; p. 9 Leemage/Universal Images Group/Getty Images; p. 11 Lynn Johnson/ National Geographic/Getty Images; p. 12 Ballista/Wikipedia.com; p. 13 Topical Press Agency/Getty Images; p. 14 David Nunuk/All Canada Photos/Getty Images; p. 15 John Zich/AFP/Getty Images; p. 17 (main) Arpad Benedek/E+/Getty Images; p. 17 (inset) Przemysław Sakrajda/Wikipedia.com; p. 18 Steve Gorton/ Dorling Kindersley/Getty Images; p. 19 Joel Arem/Photo Researchers/Getty Images; p. 20 Ron Chapple Studios/Thinkstock.com; p. 21 James L. Amos/Photo Researchers/Getty Images; p. 23 David Cupp/National Geographic/Getty Images; pp. 24, 25 David McNew/Getty Images News/Thinkstock.com; p. 26 Raph Lee Hopkins/National Geographic/Getty Images; p. 27 Sebastien Nogier/AFP/Getty Images; p. 28 Dorling Kindersley/Thinkstock.com; p. 29 Paul B. Moore/Shutterstock.com.

Printed in the United States of America

CPSIA compliance information: Batch #CS15GS: For further information contact Gareth Stevens, New York, New York at 1-800-542-2595.

CONTENTS

Words in the glossary appear in **bold** type
the first time they are used in the text.

WHAT IS A PALEONTOLOGIST?

Without fossils, we wouldn't know much about Earth's past. Fossils are created when animals and plants or their **impressions** become quickly buried by **sediment**. Over many years, the buried sediment hardens. **Minerals** in the ground replace the shell or bone of the animal or fill in the impression. These now-stone remains may be uncovered by paleontologists much, much later.

Paleontologists are scientists who use ancient remains of plants and animals to study life as it was long ago. Fossils tell stories about how plants and animals grow and change, or evolve, over millions of years. They provide clues about **geological** changes, too.

KINDS OF FOSSILS

Fossils that are formed from the remains of a plant or animal, such as a bone or shell, are called body fossils. Fossils that record an action, such as a footprint, are known as trace fossils. Some fossils may contain real bones and skin. That's because the animal was frozen in a very, very cold place.

EXAMPLES OF FOSSILS

BODY FOSSIL
- bones
- teeth
- waste

IMPRESSIONS
- scaly or bumpy skin
- feathers
- ridges and outlines of leaves

TRACE FOSSILS
- tunnels
- footprints
- resting place

Paleontologists are famous for hunting dinosaur fossils, but they also look for other animal remains as well as plant fossils.

5

DIGGING IN

If you've ever searched for seashells or shark teeth on a beach, you know what a paleontologist feels like. Paleontologists spend lots of time doing field **research** that's somewhat like this. They dig through dirt, dust off bits of rock, and put the pieces of fossilized bones or impressions together to create a whole form.

DRAGONS OR DINOSAURS?

Many paleontologists think that dragons featured in so many old tales around the world were actually inspired by dinosaur bones. People were probably trying to make sense of something that no longer existed in their time. They used their imaginations to explain the strange bones as the remains of dragons.

Paleontologists also work in **laboratories**. They study fossils closely under microscopes and perform tests on them with chemicals. They may be able to discover fossils' age, the climate conditions when the animals or plants lived, and other factors to tell a story about Earth as it once was.

If you enjoy getting dirty and solving puzzles, paleontology might be the perfect career for you.

7

EARLY PALEONTOLOGISTS

People have been discovering and explaining fossils for thousands of years. When they found fossils of animals and plants they weren't familiar with, they had to make guesses about their origins. Around 540 BC, ancient Greek thinker Xenophanes (zih-NAHF-uh-neez) noticed fossils of seashells on dry land. He **hypothesized** that the land must have been underwater during an earlier period in Earth's history.

In the eleventh century, Chinese scientist Shen Kua (SHUN KWAH) proposed an early **theory** of climate change when he discovered fossilized bamboo on land that was too dry for bamboo growth. He hypothesized that the land in that area once received more rainfall.

A NEW HOBBY

In the 1700s, fossil collecting became a popular activity for both scientists and **amateurs**. During this time, scientists began to group kinds of fossils and record details about them. French scientist Georges Cuvier is called the father of paleontology. He convinced other scientists that animals can and have died out, or become extinct.

Xenophanes

Georges Cuvier, the father of paleontology, is shown here with a fossil of a fish.

TYPES OF
PALEONTOLOGISTS

Fossils can range from tiny creatures you can't see with just your eyes to giant dinosaurs. They can be as young as a few thousand years old to 3 billion years old. For that reason, paleontologists usually choose an area to focus on.

ANIMAL PALEONTOLOGISTS

Invertebrate paleontologists study animals such as insects, corals, sponges, and starfish. Vertebrate paleontologists study animals such as fish, dinosaurs, birds, and mammals. There are so many kinds, or species, of animals that it's easier to specialize in just one of these groups. However, these paleontologists may work together since fossils of many kinds of animals may be found near each other.

Micropaleontologists study microfossils, which are fossils that can only be seen with a microscope. Paleobotanists are paleontologists who study plant fossils such as wood, leaves, flowers, and seeds. Palynologists study ancient plant **pollen**. Animal paleontologists fall into two groups: invertebrate paleontologists who study animals without a backbone and vertebrate paleontologists who study animals with backbones.

Vertebrate paleontologists research amazing bones like this, but invertebrate paleontologists do important work, too. For example, 200-million-year-old invertebrate marine fossils found in the desert of Nevada tell us that parts of the state were once covered by water.

EXCITING DISCOVERIES

Many important discoveries in paleontology were made during the nineteenth and twentieth centuries. Here are some of the famous people who unearthed them.

Mary Anning was an amateur paleontologist who taught herself about the science. She first began fossil hunting as a young girl. Around 1810, Anning and her brother found an *Ichthyosaurus*, an ancient marine reptile. She later found fossils of a **pterosaur** as well as an ancient sharklike creature.

In the Gobi desert of Mongolia, Roy Chapman Andrews discovered the first fossilized dinosaur eggs in 1923. He also found new species of dinosaurs such as the *Velociraptor*. He's been called the "real Indiana Jones."

T. REX UNEARTHED!

Barnum Brown discovered the first *Tyrannosaurus rex* fossils in 1902. He was famous across the United States. When he traveled, people gathered at train stations just to see him step off the train. Brown had his own radio show in which he'd talk about dinosaurs, fossils, and his adventures.

Ichthyosaurus

13

Roland Bird rode across the United States on a motorcycle collecting dinosaur fossils for the American Museum of Natural History in New York City. In 1938, he discovered the Glen Rose Trackway, a set of dinosaur footprints in Texas that date back 107 million years.

Can you spot the dinosaur tracks in Texas's Paluxy River?

Sue Hendrickson found the most complete *Tyrannosaurus rex* skeleton yet. It's named Sue after her!

In the 1960s, John H. Ostrom theorized that some dinosaurs evolved into birds. He offered a fossil he had found of a birdlike **raptor** as proof.

Sue Hendrickson, an amateur fossil hunter, found a complete skeleton of a *Tyrannosaurus rex* in South Dakota in 1990. You can see it at the Field Museum of Natural History in Chicago, Illinois.

EXTINCTION THEORY

In 1981, famous scientist Luis Alvarez and his son, geologist Walter Alvarez, published a theory that dinosaurs became extinct after a huge space rock hit Earth. This would have resulted in tons of dust being blown into the atmosphere, blocking the sun. After a time, plants would have died, and dinosaurs could have starved to death or died from the cold.

PALEONTOLOGY EQUIPMENT

Sometimes paleontologists get lucky—a fossil may be exposed for anyone to see. However, they usually have to use many different tools to dig and dust off layers of sand and dirt around fossils. They use large rock picks, trowels, or drills to unearth fossils, and smaller picks and brushes for more gentle work. They don't want to destroy the fossils while trying to excavate, or unearth, them!

FAMILIAR TOOLS

When paleontologists dig in softer, moist sand, they use trowels, which are similar to a shovel you may have used at the beach to build a sand castle. They also use sieves to separate dirt and sand from around fossils. These look a lot like the holes found at the bottom of beach pails you may have used to collect shells.

A sieve, also called a sifter, and a hose separate dirt, rocks, and fossils.

This paleontologist works very carefully with a fossil while wearing magnifying goggles.

Whenever hammering hard rock, paleontologists wear safety glasses and gloves to protect their eyes and hands. They also carry magnifying glasses to help them to see smaller fossils.

trowel

HOW OLD?

Paleontologists use two basic methods of figuring out how old a fossil is. One is called relative dating. Fossils are found in sedimentary rock, which forms as layers, one on top of the other. Bottom layers are older than those above. So, if a fossil is found in a bottom layer, it's older than fossils found above.

Absolute dating is a way of finding a more exact date. Certain elements in rock break down at a constant rate. By measuring how much these elements have broken down, scientists can figure out how old something is.

COUNTING RINGS

Scientists can tell how old a dinosaur was when it died just by looking at the distance between the growth rings, or marks, found just below the surface of the bones.Growth rings are far apart while the animal is young and growing quickly. They form closer together as growth slows.

Finding the age of a fossil in a layer of sediment can reveal the ages of nearby fossils. Sediment layers are easy to see in this photograph.

DINOSAUR NATIONAL MONUMENT

Dinosaur National Monument is located in the mountains between Colorado and Utah. Paleontologist Earl Douglass discovered fossils there in 1909. The remains date back 150 million years! One steep mountain wall is known as "Dinosaur Wall" because it contains fossils of about 400 dinosaurs. More than 1,500 bones remain in place but have been exposed for viewing through reliefing, which means paleontologists chipped away surrounding rock.

It's thought that the dinosaurs didn't die here. Their remains were probably carried here by water. In 1915, President Woodrow Wilson established the area as a national monument to protect its fossils and other features.

NOT BABIES, JUST SMALL

Since 1998, over 1,000 dinosaur fossils have been found in the Harz Mountains of Germany. At first, paleontologists thought they were baby dinosaur fossils. Now they think they're the smallest species of dinosaurs ever found—*Europasaurus*. There are still many discoveries to be made about prehistoric life.

Welcome to DINOSAUR, COLORADO Gateway to DINOSAUR NATIONAL MONUMENT

This is Dinosaur National Monument. Some other popular locations for paleontology digs in North America are in South Dakota, Montana, Utah, Alaska, and parts of Mexico.

TIME TO STUDY

Paleontologists study a variety of sciences in college, such as geology, biology, and **chemistry**. All can aid future work.

Geology is the study of Earth, especially of rocks, soil, and minerals and the processes they undergo. Biology is the study of life processes. Since paleontology deals with forms of life trapped within Earth's geologic formations, you can understand why both these sciences would be important to a paleontologist's work. Studying the chemical makeup of bones and shells can help paleontologists learn about Earth's climate and other factors of the environment during the time the animal was alive.

PICK A MAJOR

Most college students who plan to go into paleontology choose a biology major or geology major—or both! Micropaleontologists and invertebrate paleontologists usually have a degree in geology. Paleobotanists often major in a field of biology that deals with plants, called botany. Vertebrate paleontologists may focus on a field of biology called zoology, which is the study of animals.

Whatever your paleontological specialty, you'll need to take other courses in school to be a well-rounded scientist.

Almost all paleontologists go to graduate school. There, studies continue in the classroom as well as in laboratories. Classes do fieldwork, too. To receive a graduate degree, paleontology students complete research projects guided by a teacher and write a very long paper explaining what they've discovered. Often, this paper is published. After that, students choose their career path.

IN HIGH SCHOOL

If you like science, enjoy the outdoors, and love solving mysteries, paleontology might be the perfect career for you. When you get to high school, try to take as many advanced science classes as you can. It's also helpful to learn German, French, Russian, or Chinese, because research papers are often published in these languages. You may travel in the future, too!

A researcher removes a plaster cast from a tusk of a Columbian mammoth found near Los Angeles, California. It's likely more than 10,000 years old.

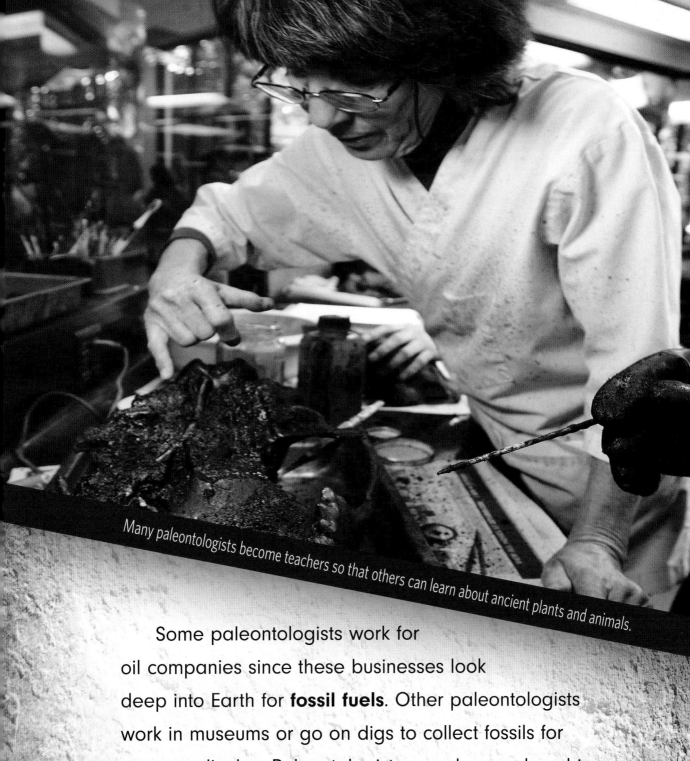

Many paleontologists become teachers so that others can learn about ancient plants and animals.

Some paleontologists work for oil companies since these businesses look deep into Earth for **fossil fuels**. Other paleontologists work in museums or go on digs to collect fossils for museum display. Paleontologists are also employed to do research and fieldwork for the government.

Even after school, paleontologists still have to keep up with the latest methods in their field. Machines called Geiger counters are used to locate elements underground often found in bones. Other machines send sound waves into the ground. If the waves bounce back in a certain way, paleontologists know something might be buried there.

There aren't a lot of paleontologists—about 3,000 in the United States. Therefore, even fewer paleontologists are experts in their field. Only about 100 around the world focus on dinosaurs, and just 40 of these actually go out on digs. It can be hard to get a job in paleontology, but those who do really love their work.

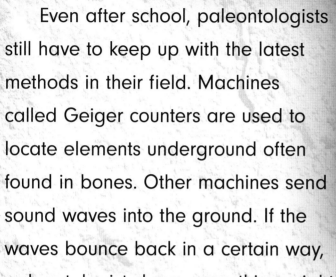

Geiger counter

One paleontologist said that going on a dig was like "being in a giant sandbox doing a jigsaw puzzle and going on a scavenger hunt all at the same time."

27

BE A PALEONTOLOGIST NOW

Luckily, you don't have to be a professional paleontologist to go on digs. Some museums put on digs that amateur paleontologists are welcome to join. The National Park Service also has a Junior Paleontologist Program, which can help you start learning about this science now.

Mary Anning began collecting fossils along the seashore when she was just a young girl. Paleontologist Jack Horner discovered his first dinosaur fossil when he was 8 years old. Read as much as you can about fossils and keep your eyes open when you're walking around the beach or even your backyard—you never know what you'll find!

A GOOD START

In 2008, 5-year-old Emelia Fawbert found a bone from a woolly rhinoceros—which lived 20,000 to 50,000 years ago! Emelia and her father were in Gloucestershire, England, on her very first fossil hunting trip at the time. She has decided to become a paleontologist in the future because of her experience.

Mary Anning

Many amateur paleontologists have been responsible for amazing fossil finds.

GLOSSARY

amateur: someone who does something without pay

chemistry: a science that deals with the structure and properties of matter and the changes it goes through

fossil fuel: matter formed over millions of years from plant and animal remains that is burned for power

geological: having to do with the science of Earth as recorded in rocks

hypothesize: to use known facts to suggest an explanation for an event or set of conditions

impression: a mark left as a result of applying pressure on something

laboratory: a place with tools to perform experiments

mineral: matter in the ground that forms rocks

pollen: a fine yellow dust produced by plants

pterosaur: one of a group of flying dinosaurs

raptor: a small or medium-sized dinosaur that ate other dinosaurs

research: studying to find something new

sediment: matter, such as stones and sand, that is carried onto land or into the water by wind, water, or land movement

theory: an explanation based on facts that is generally accepted by scientists

FOR MORE INFORMATION

BOOKS

Gray, Susan H. *Paleontology: The Study of Prehistoric Life.* New York, NY: Children's Press, 2012.

McGowan, Chris. *Dinosaur Discovery: Everything You Need to Be a Paleontologist.* New York, NY: Simon & Schuster Books for Young Readers, 2011.

WEBSITES

Fossil Facts
www.sciencekids.co.nz/sciencefacts/earth/fossils.html
Read more about fossils and how they form.

Junior Paleontologist Program
www.nature.nps.gov/geology/nationalfossilday/jrpaleo.cfm
Find out more about the Junior Paleontologist Program at the National Park Service.

Paleontology
www.amnh.org/explore/ology/paleontology
Check out what the American Museum of Natural History has to say about paleontology.

INDEX